The R.E.A.L.

(Reality...Evolution...And Life)

Compiled by:

Cassandra Edwards and The A & T Four Middle College

at N.C. A & T State University

American Literature Students Spring 2023

Copyright @2023 Cassandra Edwards

All rights reserved. Printed in the United States of America. No parts of this publication may be reproduced, distributed, or transmitted in any form or by any means, without prior written permission of the copyright owner, except for the use of brief quotations in a book review.

Words from the teacher:

"The Sky Is Not My Limit, I can soar beyond the clouds."
-Cassandra Edwards

This quote first came to me when I was a senior in high school. Struggling to find a way to open my college essay my English teacher said to me, "The sky is the limit you can do anything." Although I appreciated her words, I looked her square in the face and said, "The sky is not my limit, I can soar beyond the clouds." Ever since then that has been my motto. I instill these words in the children who I teach in the classroom and when I became a mother into my own child. There are no limits that even the sky itself can place on someone who believes they are limitless. I am limitless and my life is a living testimony of just that.

The limits that were placed upon me as a young child by society, by family, and even by myself have since been removed. I removed them! I changed my mindset, I shifted the direction I was headed in, and I deliberately became intentional about the words I spoke and the things I believed.

Looking back on all my personal hardships I see how much they have affected me. I realize that during these times I allowed myself to stop progression. I halted all things that could help me, allowing the harshness of my life to condemn me. Yet now that I look back at these times I realize I had the potential all along to break out of it. I realize that my wings never stopped working. I just refused to use them.

This book is dedicated to all of the students, not just in this class, who have learned to use their pen to speak the words their mouths can not say. To those who have trusted the process even when it made no sense to them.

My hope is that they will never stop writing and never let society silence them ever again.

We Wear The Mask (A Collaborative Poem)

Inspired by Paul Laurence Dunbar's Poem

We wear the mask that hides us from the outside world
I wear the mask of a motherless child who lost her mom as a young girl
We wear the mask that hides our truth
I wear a mask that shields me from others who feel I have something to prove
We wear the mask that hides us from being something great
I wear the mask to keep me from stepping out of my comfort zone to see my fate
We wear the mask that hides our past
I wear the mask that makes my happiness last
We wear the mask that hides our potential
I wear the mask that shows that my knowledge is substantial
We wear the mask that hides our smile

I wear the mask that boosts my confidence for a while

We wear the mask that hides the real us on social media sites

I wear the mask that shows my true colors in person of who I am inside

We wear the mask now to protect ourselves

I wear a mask to enhance my health

We wear the mask to hide our weaknesses from others

I wear the mask to avoid trouble

We wear the mask to hide from our fears

I wear the mask to hold back my tears

We wear the mask to hide our shame

I wear the mask so nobody can see me go insane

We wear the mask to tell our story

I wear the mask to tell my glory

We wear the mask to show who others want us to be

I wear the mask to show that I can only be me.

Letters to Our Mothers

In this section we pay tribute to our mothers and those who have served as mothers in our lives.

"A mother's hug lasts long after she lets go." - Unknown

Dear Momma,

It may not seem like I appreciate it but, I just want you to know that you are my everything. You are a literal walking miracle and for that I am grateful. I am thankful for you, your life, health, and strength, and for sticking with me through everything. I love you and I will always cherish you.

Love always,
Keith

Dear Mother,

I would like to start off by saying thank you. I appreciate everything you have done for me up to this point in my life. You have done so much for me and taught me so much over these last sixteen years. Even as a young boy, you raised me to be the young man I am today. Now that I am coming of age, you are still teaching me how to become a young man and helping me transfer the skills that will help me provide for myself and those I love. Even though I do not show how much I love and appreciate you every day, you are embedded in my heart and will never leave. I could not ask for a better mother. I thank God that he made me your son and I am truly grateful for him giving you not just life but the power and strength to raise me. Again, I thank you for everything you have done in my life and the things you will do in the future. Thank you, Mother.
Love,
Colin

Dear Mother,

I hope that you are doing well right now. Thank you for everything you have done and continue to do now. I am sorry for all the times that I may have let you down or disappointed you. I love you and know you want what is best for me and my life. I know that you are always there when I need you because you have been in the past. I will forever be thankful for you.

Love,
Matthew

Dear Mother,

You are my biggest supporter! Whenever I was low, it was your call that perked me up and made my day. A conversation with you was enough to fill my heart with happiness. You are such a positive and cheerful person! No matter what I have done, you have always loved me for the person I am. I wonder how you could easily manage such a stubborn little child like me. I am glad you love me so much.

Love,
Jameil

Dear Ma,

I know that sometimes I may be difficult and hard for you to deal with, but I love you. You were always there for me even when nobody else was. You show me how to be myself and that I am special. Words don't express how much you mean to me, and how thankful I am for what you have done for me. I LOVE YOU MA!

Love,
Tyree

Dear Mama,

I know I don't show it enough, but I love you. I want to thank you for working so hard for me to have a roof over my head, nice clothes on my back, and shoes on my feet. I thank you for getting along with my dad to ensure me and my sister have a father in our life. You are loving, funny, honest, loyal, and beautiful. There is much more I can say but words cannot explain how amazing you are. You support me in everything I do and cheer loudly and proudly for every accomplishment I make as if it's your own. I can't wait till I get to the age where I can take care of you because you deserve it. I love you Ma.

Sincerely,
Franklin

Dear Mom,

You've been such a high influence on my life. I couldn't ask for a better and more wonderful person other than you. I may not say it as much, but God knows I truly appreciate you for all that you've done for me. You've helped me through tough times and through times where I've needed guidance and assistance. There is no one more extraordinary and incredible than you. If it weren't for you, I wouldn't have grown up to be the young man I am today. I wouldn't dare trade you for anyone else. You're perfect just the way you are. I love you Mom and I thank you so much for being there for me.

Sincerely,
Tyler

Dear Ma,

Even though I don't say it as much, you are the backbone in my life. You fight all my battles beside me and give me honest advice even when I don't think I need it. You birthed me, bathed me, fed me, and raised me. You give me things I want and need in life. You make sure I always have a smile on my face. You chastised me when needed and made sure I knew right from wrong. Most of all, you helped shape me. I just want to thank you for all the things you have done for me and I love you ma.

Love,
Ross III

Dear Mom,

Even though you already know you're my favorite person I want you to know I love you a lot. For all the times in the world where I needed help you were there for me. Throughout my life you have always had my back and supported me in all I do. I don't really have much to say but I love you a lot mom.

Sincerely,
Nadir

Dear Mom,

I know we are not in the best condition right now, but I want you to know that I'm trying my best and I am getting better. I know I can be difficult, but I am working hard on not causing you stress and worry. I'll continue to do my best for you. All of your sacrifices since before I was born will not be in vain. I am thankful for you persevering through life. There's no mother like you. Je t'Aime.

Love,
Joseph

"A Mother's Love" by Cassandra Edwards

A mother's love is one of genuine care and concern
A special type of feeling for which we all one day yearn
It is a love like no other than can be felt
And one that reassures us that we are perfect as our own genuine self
A mother's love can be felt near and from afar
But the best thing about a mother's love is that it serves as a guard
A guard against all the evil in the world that tries to consume us
And against the heartache that we will one day experience that will betray our trust
A mother's love will shield us from the hurt and pain
And give us the strength to go on and love again

Just Like My Daddy
(OR NOT)

In life, many of us have all been told at some point or have heard the phrase in public "you are just like your daddy." This can be a good or a bad thing and honestly some of us are nothing like our daddies. That also can be a good or bad thing. In this section we focus on our fathers, or the lack thereof, in order to show appreciation for who they are/were. Our goal is to thank them for the lessons we learned because of who they were or were not in our lives.

Nothing Like My Daddy by Cassandra Edwards

I am nothing like my daddy, not just because I am a girl
But because I would never let anything keep me from being the center of my child's world
Nothing like my daddy because he had a habit that he could not beat
Others saw strength, while I believed he was weak
He abandoned us and created a new family
So being like my daddy has never been a dream for me
They say I am just like my daddy with his high cheeks and smile
But I prayed to never be like my daddy who left us for a long while
Just like my daddy because we have the same hustle and grind
But nothing like him because for my family I will always have time
I realize I am more like my daddy than I wish to admit

Because when the odds stacked against him, he never quit
If being like my daddy was what I wanted to be
I'd request that his strength be passed down to me

Sort of Like My Daddy by Tyler Cooper

I am like my daddy in a few ways.

Many things like facial features are not to be praised.

Some emotions are left to be thought about.

Even so our lives may travel different routes.

To be honest, while he is, I am not really all that social.

My dad, on the other hand, is pretty negotiable.

It takes a bit of time for me to be able to lock in.

While I don't, my daddy needs time to make amends.

I know I am just like my daddy when it comes to this-

Me and my daddy are definitely known for taking risks.

Just Like My Dad by Franklin Brown Jr.

Just like my dad cause I have his name

I think a lot like my dad

I'm chill, calm, and collective like my dad

I will be a strong, African American man like my dad

I'm funny and athletic just like my dad

I don't get my drip from my dad, but I can cook like him

I don't want to be just like my dad,

But I'll take some characteristics from him and make them better

When I get old, I'll provide for my family just like my dad

But I'll make better decisions than he did

I will fight through adversity and learn from my mistakes

Just Like My Dad

Just My Father by Colin Burgess

I appreciate my father however

I do not want to be like him...nope, not never

I thank him for all he has done while being here

But I still need to know where he was over the years

I am glad he wanted to come back

In hopes that we can get our relationship back on track

Over my life I have grown

I learned many things from what my father has shown

Even though bonding gets hard sometimes

I hope things continue to get better overtime

Although I am not just like my father in any way

I appreciate my father for who he is today

Just Like My Daddy by Keith Bradley

I want to be like my dad to a certain degree

I want to be a hard-working man just like my dad

I want to be able to live up to expectations like my dad

But I want to be a better role model than my dad

I want to be a good father like my dad

But I don't want to be like my dad

I don't want to pick up the same bad habits he has

I will achieve all my goals in life

I won't be in the same situation he's in

I don't want to be just like my day

I want to be better than my dad

Just Like My Dad by Tyree Brown

Just like my Dad

I'm strong just like my Dad

I'm smart just like my Dad

I'm caring just like my Dad

I'm giving just like my Dad

I'm myself just like my Dad

I'm confident just like my Dad

I'm an extrovert just like my Dad

But I won't abandon my kids like my real dad

Just Like My Dad by Joseph Weah

Just like my dad

My name is just like my dads

I look just like my dad

I am strong just like my dad

But I am smarter than my dad

I am jolly unlike my dad

I am healthy unlike my dad

I will be a better spouse than my dad

I will be different from my dad

Just Like My Dad by Nadir Stukes

Just like my dad

I'm intelligent like my dad

I look like my dad

I'm taller than my dad

I maintain my life like my dad

I get my work done like my dad

I wish to be hard working like my dad

I love my dad

Where I am From

This next section of poems follows the model of the poem "Where I am From" by George Ella Lyon. We decided to explore the origins of where we are from following her template.

Where I'm From by Cassandra Edwards

I am from itchy plaid blankets on a twin bed

From my own phone line at thirteen and my mom's 89 Mustang

I am from "Close my door and don't let anyone in this house"

I am from a two-family flat with adjoining doors

And a vacant lot on the side where we turned flips on abandoned mattresses

I am from planting watermelons

Whose seeds never grew from the ground

I am from Extension cords and Hot combs

From Colleen and George

And from broken homes and kids raising kids

From skating on Saturdays

I am from church every Sunday and Wednesdays too

From fried chicken and spaghetti with hot dogs

From my mother hosting all the holiday parties

And from her passing away when I was nineteen

From college broughs in every color

I am from the moments when I didn't think I would make it out

And other moments when I knew I had no other option

Where I Am From by Bernard Ross

I am from a Lightning Mcqueen bedroom set

From Benjamin Bear cd`s and my father's Grand Marquis

I am from the one-story house

And a big lake and an oak tree

I am from the three big palm trees in my front yard

Whose coconuts were always falling off the tree

I am from Winnie the Pooh and hot wheels

From Jackie and Deborah

And from strict attitudes and peaceful minds

From popcorn and washing the car on Saturday

I am from my Lord and Savior Jesus Christ

From sweet potato pie and brown stew chicken

From visiting my Great Grandmother

And from laughing with my aunt

From getting my first power wheel

I am from the moments I spent under those palm trees

And from moments of Bernard Ross II

Where I Am From by Tyree Brown

I am from DJ the stuffed dog

From Arm N Hammer toothpaste and cocoa butter lotion

I am from "Jamal bring your tail in here"

And a small two-bedroom apartment with crayon drawings all over the walls

I am from leaves blowing into my house at any moment

Whose flying would spread all throughout the house

I am from Incredible Hulk punching gloves and a little red Honda with no AC

From the Coopers and the Browns

And from arguing aunties and loud, little cousins

From always shopping and going places

I am from Grandparents who were Pastors

From baked Mac N Cheese and oatmeal with ham slices

From spending every weekend with my Grandma

And from falling on a brick at my Granny's house

From killing my pet fish with a soccer ball

I am from moments that make you who you are and learning it the hard way

And from time spent with a crazy and loving family

Where I'm From by Joseph Weah

I am from video games and nature

From Vaseline and cartoon characters

I am from small apartments

Moving back and forth

I am from a tree that timbered

Whose trunk was struck by lightning

I am from a hard comb and buzz cuts

From Martha and Joseph

And from forgiveness and kindness

From joining a soccer club

I am from Thanksgiving

From acheke and fufu

From a victim to war

And from good grades and scores

A stuffed donald duck

I am from the moments of myself

And moments with Martha and Joseph

Where I am From by Tyler Cooper

I am from a place of health and interest

From Dinosaurs and Computers

I am from a unique set of structures

And a fortified set of plains

I am from a rose of peace and beauty

Whose leaves are thin

I am from toys that are small and noisy

From my father and my mother

And from a nice mother and an intelligent father

From my Grandmother being courteous and my

Grandfather being hard-working

I am from a Christian home

From fried chicken and macaroni and cheese

From World War II

And from being a Farmer

From the time when I burned my hand on the stove

I am from the moments of life

Where I am From by Nadir Stukes

I am from wall-e sheets

From Kirkland water and a Ford F-150

I am from a big home on a hill

and several rooms

I am from apple trees whose apples fall unlike Ben

Simmons jump shot

I am from an Xbox One and thick glasses

From Stukes and Johnson

And from loving, caring, and happiness

I am from super bowl parties

From jalapeno poppers and steak

I am from winning championships

And from gathering to celebrate

From my favorite tiny yellow bus

I am from the moments of happiness

And the moments of Nadir Stukes

Just a Little Poetry

In this section we experimented with writing poetry. It was a struggle formulating thoughts, deciding if we would make them rhyme, following formats and guidelines, but we hope you enjoy the poems we produced. Maybe, just maybe, there is a poet locked on the inside.

Haikus by Zackary Singletary

Sports
I love basketball
Lebron James is my favorite
He is the greatest

Food
Pizza is my favorite
We all need food for protein
Food is good for you

School
School is important
Everybody needs school to learn stuff
School is required

Music
Hip Hop is the best
Juice World is my favorite
He was a legend

Clothing
I love wearing crocs
I have a lot of black clothes
Black clothes are the best

Haikus by Colin Burgess

Sports
I love to play sports
I enjoy multiple sports
I am athletic

Food
I can be picky
Bacon is in my top tier
Love me some french fries

School
School can be boring
I'm not a big fan of school
Assignments really suck

Music
My music calms me
I listen to R&B
I'm lost in music

Clothing
My clothes express me
I am into wearing shoes
Big fan of nice shoes

Haikus by Keith Bradley

Sports
I'm a hurdler
My favorite sport is track
I love running track

Food
I love to eat food
I love to eat healthy foods
I love fried chicken

School
I do not like school
School brings nothing but headaches
You will gain nothing

Music
I always play music
J. Cole is the best artist
Music calms my nerves

Clothing
I love to dress up
I always match my outfits
My shoe game crazy

Haikus by Tyler Cooper

Sports
I don't play baseball
I used to but haven't tried
It wouldn't be cool

Food
I love me some food
I can't wait to be fed some food
Food is so good for me

School
I dislike school bad
My favorite class is science
I hate math truly

Music
I love the song alone
It makes me feel so at home
I enjoy the song

Clothing
I'm not into clothes
I like them but not that much
They are still really nice

Haikus by Nadir Stukes

Basketball
I like basketball
I play all five positions
I want to play now

Food
Food is the best
Without food, I cannot live life
Give me food now

Music
Music lives inside me
Music flows through my bones always
I really love music

Haikus by Joseph Weah

Futball
Futbal beautiful
Great futballers all around
Messi is the best

Food
I eat peach and cake
Fruit is good for your body
We love good health

School
Junior year hardest
ACT SAT hard
I will get through it

Music
Kali Uchis good
Spotify I listen to
Music helps me live

Clothing
Clothing looks so swell
Suits are great for formal clothes
Tempted to buy more

Haikus by Franklin Brown

Sports
Basketball is fun
Winning games is key for me
It's a mental game

Food
Pizza is greasy
Grapes give off sweet juice everyday
I eat food everyday

School
Bookbags are heavy
I sleep on my desk everyday
I sharpen pencils

Music
Playboi carti fan
Music helps me live when bored
Music is Future

Clothing
Designer off white
I wear comfortable clothes
Balenciaga

Haiku Poems by Matthew Lee

Sports
Football is real fun
Wrestling is also fun too
Sports are the best thing

Food
Food is the best thing
It is best to eat healthy
I love to eat steak

School
School is important
School can set you up for life
School gives you knowledge

Music
Music is calming
I love Christian music too
Music can be good

Clothing
Clothes are important
You need clothes for comfort too
Clothes keep you real warm

Love by Tyler Cooper

Love is truly a remarkable thing

Love to me is like a red rose

There are specific types to the rose as well

You have the center, the thorns, the leaves, and the stem

Some problems and goals, all in one

It takes time and effort to understand them

Sometimes it even takes a bit of courage

To truly understand a person, you must gain their trust

Even at dark times you both may go through

The love for each other is a definite must

Love by Franklin Brown

Love changes your mindset

Love is what some people live for

I look for love

My mom loves me

My dad loves me

My sister loves me

I love my family

I love basketball

I love to listen to music

One thing I can't forget is that God Loves me

Love by Nadir Stukes

Love is untrustworthy

Love is not always for everyone

Love can be a test

If you can trust the one you love you won't stress

With less stress, you can better yourself

Love is a burning flame

Sometimes it burns out, sometimes it lives

It warms our soul everyday

And keeps up going all the time

It's a bond that keeps us close.

Love by Keith Bradley

What is love?

Love is a feeling from above

Love is something that the even the rigid feel

But how do you know if it's real?

Love is kind

It brings a certain sense to the mind

Love is an emotion

It makes you feel seasick

Like you're on the ocean

But what is love?

Love is the unknown

Love by Zackary Singletary

Love is a beautiful thing

Love is something you should take pride in

Love is something that is an essential part of life

Love is an experience

Love is a part of us all

Love is earned

Love is a privilege

Love shouldn't be taken for granted

Unless it will fall apart

Love by Joseph Weah

Love is lovely when it's forever

Should we all love? Many waver

So shall I?

I focus for better

Until I am tender

For less chance of my chest being torn asunder

When in love are you in your right mind?

Or is your lover causing you to make ridiculous misunderstandings?

Motherly love everyone yearns for

Maybe you will find that until they close the door

Love Poem by Colin Burgess

Love is everything

Love is what people want

But is something people seek

Love is nothing

Love is something no one desire

But something to people that is weak

Love is mental

Love is something we dream of

But something that is like a long streak

Love is everything

Love Is by Cassandra Edwards

Love is feeling that consumes and overtakes us
A feeling that makes us be vulnerable with those we may not even fully trust
Love is something we all desire and need at a given time
A feeling that makes us want to lose our minds
Unconditional love is the best type to feel
Superficial love is one that is not real
We all need love and we should be able to show it too
The one thing about love is it should always be true
Love is the one thing that will keep us going in life
When you want to give up you will stick around and fight
Love is ...

Love Poem by Matthew Lee

What is love?

A feeling shared by those most cared for

A feeling too sacred to describe

A feeling that brings out more

A feeling that leaves nothing to hide

A feeling that could be hard to express

A feeling that can be good or bad

A feeling that can make you stress

A feeling that some never had

A feeling that can leave you happy

A feeling that can make you change

A feeling that can be really snappy

A feeling that can be really strange

Some people will never understand the true meaning of love

It's a feeling that we all receive from our God in heaven above

Free to Be Me by Keith Bradley Jr.

Free to be me

Live a long life just like a tree

No more hiding, no more pretending

No more conforming to society's endless mending

No longer bound by others' expectations

I am liberated, free from all limitations

Free to speak the truth

To inspire the youth

Free to be me

Let me live my life in 2023

Free to Be Me by Franklin Brown

Free to be me

I am free to be me because of my rights

I am free to be me because of my family

I am free to be me because of my ancestors

I am free to be me because I am a smart brown boy

I am free to be me on social media

I am free to be me on the basketball court

I am free to be me at concerts

I am free to be me in the month of February

I am free to be me in school

I am free to be me because I am god's child

Free to Be Me by Joseph Weah

There are norms and regulations

In every society some things may be known as odd

Although you should be normal to yourself

The way you think, and talk should be normal to you

Because in other locations of the world they may be viewed otherwise

If someone has an Italian accent and moves to America, their accent may be viewed as unusual

Everybody is precepted as peculiar somewhere

So why not just be peculiar everywhere

Your in-group will always be someone's out-group

Although you are not completely free to be yourself everywhere.

Free to Be Me by Nadir Stukes

Free as a bird that soars in the sky
With wings outstretched and spirits high
No worries to weigh me down
Just the wind, the sun, and the ground.

Free to dream to hope to be
To wander or wonder to see
The world in all its grandeur and glory
And write my own unique story
I'll write it to show all my glory
Hopefully I won't end up like Finding Dory.

Free to Be Me by Tyree Brown

Free to be me.

Free to express my emotion.

Free to be me.

Free to love who I want.

Free to be me.

Free to be in my own skin.

Free to be me.

Free to show my creativity.

Free to be me.

Free to be who I want, how I want, where I want.

Free to Be Me by Tyler Cooper

How can I be free to be me?

Because greatness is all I see.

I can achieve one step at a time,

and I am willing and able to reach and climb.

I believe nothing can contain me;

my future is all I foresee.

I know if I make one step; then I am carried three.

The effort is all mine, with the ability to shine.

I desire hopes of happiness and peace of mind.

When I plant my feet to win the race of life, I shall strive and win a significant prize.

So here I go, reaching high above the great blue sky.

And all you will be able to say, "Look at the young man grow, my, my, my."

Don't hinder me, don't ignore me, I am somebody, treat me with dignity.

How can I be free? Watch me soar and be the best me I can be.

Free to Be Me by Bernard Ross III

Free to be me

To be in my own skin

To like what I like

To do Ross

Free to be me

To have my own thoughts

To have my own words

Because I'm the Boss

Free to be me

And only me

I'm free to be

Me

Free to Be Me by Colin Burgess

I am thankful for having two sisters and being me

Now we added four kids, more boys that is three

At first it I was quiet, and I was the youngest

I was the small one but now I am the biggest

Living between spilt houses, but mainly with my mom

I know both houses like the back of my palm

I am a student athlete that plays two sports

Baseball and hooping on the court

I love me some music and jamming out

With listening to R&B without a doubt

Author Bios

Keith Bradley, born and raised in Greensboro, North Carolina, is a caring and compassionate person who enjoys lending a helping hand. He is a senior at A&T Four Middle College at N. C. A&T State University who enjoys socializing with his friends and family. Keith a talented individual with a promising future. He is a multi-sport athlete and participates in football and track. Keith is currently a dual-enrolled student who aspires to work as a physical therapist and a professional athlete. Photgraphy is a hobby he has recently picked up.

Franklin Brown was born in Greensboro ,North Carolina but has lived in the neighboring city of High Point his entire life. From a young age, he has always enjoyed playing basketball. When he isn't playing basketball, he is either listening to music or playing a game. Both music and his family are extremely important to him. Franklin also enjoys eating and trying new foods. His dream is to either play in the NBA or start his own private equity firm. Franklin is ready to break out of his shell and talk about real issues. He is excited to see how teens and others respond to his writing.

Tyree Brown was born in Charleston, South Carolina and moved to Greensboro, North Carolina at the age of six. Tyree has always had an extravagant mind as a child and discovered his true passions later in life. These passions includes music, crafts, and learning new things about the world. He is a hands-on learner and can often be found building and crafting. He can usually be spotted with headphones listening to tunes. It is his love for creativity and learning that he wants to share with the world.

Colin Burgess was born in Greensboro, North Carolina into a family of two sisters. Being the only boy raised in a household of women, he spent a lot of time playing by himself. When he got older, his family adopted four children to their family, so now Colin has three sisters and three brothers. He has always been the positive one in the family and is usually optimistic about anything he does or sees. Colin is very goofy and is always smiling no matter what he does. If he is not smiling or bouncing around then he is more than likely exhausted. Colin also loves listening to music as it is calming to him. More recently, Colin has been intrigued by sneakers and allows them to show his individuality.

Tyler Cooper was born in Greensboro, North Carolina. He was a preemie at birth and endured bullying from kindergarten to seventh grade. He turned what was a negative situation into a positive solution. After touring Greensboro Urban Ministry in his seventh-grade year, he discovered there were people in need of a hot meal and a warm bed. He started a monthly food drive and has collected over seven thousand pounds of food. He now serves as a board member of the Directors at Greensboro Urban Ministry, is involved with YMCA Achievers Leadership, N.C. A&T Upward Bound, Greensboro Youth Council, and Greensboro Urban Ministry Volunteers. He motto is "We do better; then we can be better." He has a passion and desire to become a Computer Science Engineer.

Cassandra Edwards is an English Teacher at A&T Four Middle College at North Carolina A&T State University in Greensboro, NC. A native of St. Louis, MO, she is a mother of one daughter. She began writing poetry at the age of eleven and published her debut novel *Unsolicited Tears* in 2019. She has since published *Before the Ink Dries* (2021), **Poetic Prayers** (2022), **Cassie Can Count**, the first of a children's series (2022), joined in on several anthologies, and has produced several other books with students from Winston Salem and Greensboro, NC.

Jameil Henry was born in Asheville, North Carolina and moved to Browns Summit where he has lived most of his life. He is a money driven guy who is always figuring out ways to work and make money so that he can save up for his future. He appreciates school and the teachers that do their job. He has a few close friends and tries to maintain a humble lifestyle. He is his mother's only child, but one of many on his father side. He wants to help motivate young black men to get money and would like to educate them on the ways to do so. He is eager to share his knowledge and power with his peers and others.

Matthew Lee was born and raised in Greensboro, North Carolina and continues to live there to this day. He loves to volunteer and hang out at his church because it provides him with happiness. He also plays football and wrestling for Northern Guilford High School. He often feels misunderstood though he is surrounded by so many people who care. He struggles to find himself on his walk as a Christian but also as a developing young man. He often finds himself making mistakes and hopes that he can turn things around soon. He hopes that he can use writing as an outlet for being a better version of himself.

Bernard Ross was born in Miami, Florida where he lived until the age of five. After moving to North Carolina, he developed an interest in cars and building things. He is extremely ambitious and has big goals for himself. He comes from a wise family. He is very smart and articulate and wants to become a mechanical engineer. Bernard relies on creativity and skill to get through his day, especially through music. He goes by the name Ross and is ready to take the world by storm.

Zackary Singletary, born and raised in Philadelphia, Pennsylvania, is now a senior at A&T Four Middle College at N.C. A&T State University. He is an aspiring entrepreneur who is eager to learn from those who came before him. Zackary is a young man who wants to follow his dreams though he can be very indecisive at times. He is determined to persevere through whatever trials and tribulations he may face and is self-motivated. He tries to make sure he stays optimistic and level-headed. Zackary is also extremely articulate and enjoys thinking through situations and not making decisions under impulse. He not only wants to see change but is also willing to do the "dirty work" that many people are not willing to do to see change. He is a great leader who does what is needed to be successful.

Nadir Stukes was born in Florence, South Carolina and has lived in Summerfield, North Carolina most of his life. As a senior, Nadir has been successful in his short life. He has always been a creative and intelligent young man looking for his chance to impact the world. His current dream is to run track at the professional level or play basketball. Although he struggles with managing his time, he always tries to stay organized. He is ready to share his story.

Joseph Weah was born in Greensboro, North Carolina, but his family is from Monrovia, Liberia, West Africa. At a young age he developed a love for futball and playing videos games. He enjoys watching professional players and is fascinated by the way they move, the way they think, and the way they deal with the situation they are in during the game. Joseph listens to music during most of his daily activities such as walking, eating, talking to friends, and more. His dream would be to make a living off what he loves to do. He wants to travel back to his country with his mother. Although his humor and lively personality are normally hidden, he hopes to one day be recognized for them both.

Made in the USA
Middletown, DE
23 December 2023

44903530R10044